Allow yourself
to feel it in
your heart.
When you're
through, pass
it on ♡

For

the soulful women in my life,

Each of you gave me a little more meaning – thank you.

For little me,

You are everything you've imagined to be– so imagine beautiful things.

For love,

I run towards you with my palms open. You are in my blood.

The Heart of the Pomegranate,
Words are just words but –
The deeper the red **Of** your hues,
The more I know you have to offer to me
For what is the fruit
Without the running flow of your soul and **Seed**?
For what are the branches **And** roots of your tree,
If they do not hold you close nor dance in the **Wind** with your leaves.
For what is the creation of life,
If I do not have the passion to create.

Table of Contents

The Woman —

Dear Strange Man —

Godspeed, My Love —

Introduction

Dear Reader,
I present to you a piece of work that comes deeply from the heart.
The heart of a woman who has a lot to give,
so thank you for receiving.
This book is divided into three parts with
each part showcasing an important part of the cycle
as thinkers, lovers, etc.
Each chapter is a compilation of writing that blends the art of poetry and vulnerable thoughts.
'The Woman' is about coming into your own space as one and the journey it takes to understand the power we have.
'Dear Strange Man' is about childhood wounds, love, fulfillment and pain.
'Godspeed, my love' is about faith, hope, and the innate feeling we as humans have for believing in a Creator.
You certainly do not have to be a poet or religious to open this book,
I would just ask that you are curious.
I would consider this piece of work an experience for my readers.
I hope that when you are through with this book, you will see that you are a powerful person in which all good things on Earth may find a home through.

The Woman–

[We are the roots, the stem, the leaves, the petals and the fruit.]

نحن الجذور نحن الجذع ونحن الأوراق ونحن الثمره

ہم جڑیں، تنا، پتے، پنکھڑی اور پھل ہیں۔

If tomorrow our sky is no longer blue–
And the clouds make it known that they are grieving and hungry for her,
And the crows caw from the bottom of their bellies with great mourning that is to be heard acres away;
Just know that although she is not physically among our birds and mountains,
Our trees or rocks,
She is here in deep spirit.
If tomorrow our sky is no longer blue–
I am sure the clouds will make their grief and hunger for her known through the sound of dark light.
To know that there was a time in which man believed
that he created the phenomenon of thunder and lighting is humiliating.
The clouds roar and crash in the name of every woman lost.
The clouds shake and cry when they would see her sad so imagine when she was gone,
How dark the sky had been.
They wept for her,
They were hungry for her,
They cried out to her putting on a show on Earth,
flooding valleys,
striking down trees,
shaking rocks with their thunder–
but she was resting beneath the Earth.
A single tear from an infant cloud found its way down a mountain,
through the bedrock,
and buried itself in her casket.

Oh, to have nature itself weep for one of its own.

—

If the stars ever saw her ashes, if the planets saw what became of her—
They would weep.
If Jupiter and her moons, the sun, the dead and undead lights of the universe experienced or were a witness to the sight of her burning,
They would weep as well.
It would be raining from the heavens.
I was told by the Earth that if I were to see her ashes close up,
they would be the image of the universe all colliding, expanding, birthing – existing.
We are the stars, we are stardust – but she was the first.
It will be of no surprise if the stars were too crafted from clay.
Heaven's clay.
They found nebulas, constellations, power, grace, galaxies, and life in her ashes.
They found worlds colliding, lights forming, lights dying, and asteroids in her remains.
What now laid as gray-black ashes was once a vessel of life for Earth.
One may ask if this is why The Woman was tasked with so much pain to carry here—
Because she already had the universe within her.
There was life and death already happening a million times inside her.
She was already used to starting over and making something beautiful after it all died in chaos.
The pattern of light and dark was in her blood.
Every part of The Woman mimics the annihilation and resurrection of a hundred worlds.
The women before her had it in their blood as well.

"She was one of us," the stars bellowed
"Let her come home to us."

And they let her ashes go—
Back home.

> **"Mama" the little one handed her a white clover weed.**
> **"What a beautiful flower, thank you my love."**
> **"Why do you protect my heart mama?" the little one laughs.**
> **"Your joy is my joy."**

A woman does not need to birth children of her own to reach
the peak of femininity,
or to experience motherhood.
A woman does not need life blown into her womb to
experience the delicacy of motherhood.
A woman does not need her blood every moon to experience
the toils and heartache that come with being a mother,
that comes with being a woman.
Motherhood is not exclusive to caring for your own blood.
It is being able to see those in need of guidance,
It is being able to give,
To love,
To rejoice at the happiness of her loved ones,
And to be humble but conscious of the power she has.

—

I did not walk through years of pain
for you to learn of my miseries and mirror them,
Or to hold it over my head
where the clouds are still raining.
You could not do the great things I have done.

You are not even half of me.

—

What they will not tell you
and what they have tried to hide
is that womanhood is made of the finest things relevant to The Human Experience.
It is made of softness, love, nurture, chaos, and strength–
Oh so much strength.
A woman who learns to flourish in the storm when she's given trials,
is a hurricane to not be reckoned with.
The Human Experience is nothing more than Hands that create their own demise,
Dismissive of elements such as kindness and wonder that femininity offers.
It's the stories of the Earth before us,
The stories, the pain and the glory that we carry on our backs,
Between our shoulders,
In our hips,
Our necks,
Our tears.
What a beautiful way for the universe to express her pain and happiness through the phenomenon of being a woman.

—

I know you are used to mania.
Daughter, may I remind you that you need to feel peace more than you feel the need for power.

They have spent much time talking of what things a girl must
look up to throughout her life,
marriage and childbirth
but the best things that really ground a woman in her prime
years
that they do not talk about
would be the support of her sisters, **blood or not**.
Blood surely is thicker than water,
but we also choose our *blood*,
who we run to in our heartbreaks,
who we mesh our *blood* moon cycles with.
Allowing our nature as women to choose who we have our
days of worship with.

Until death do us part, my flowers.

—

The woman steps into her Dark Feminine usually after she
realizes the spirit of her womb and heart are broken.
This feeling was once accompanied by the sky's show of rage
and lightning.
Powerful strikes making their way through the clouds in
shades of sorrow and beauty;
Blue, purple and red.
But–
When a woman steps into her Dark Feminine
She is not a victim or prisoner to her trials.
She is the figure waiting at the ruins of the Parthenon to take
her power back.
She is the figure waiting in the tombs of queens to be called to
begin her reign.
She is the woman watching the sea cliffs with bow and arrow
in her hand, defending all that is hers.
"Who will dare take anything from me again?"
The castles were hers.
The laughter of children were hers to cherish and make music
from.
Before,
they would tell her what the weather would be that day
But today,
She makes the weather.
It will rain if she pours milk into a golden cup.
The sun will shine if she chooses to eat honey with silver.
It will be a cloudy day if she wears her opal necklace.
You must understand the journey it took to get here,
the things that broke the spirit of her womb and heart.

—

Blood of mine, why do you teach your daughters that her completeness and freedom is dictated by the presence of a man?
Was she not born as a whole?
Blood of mine, why do you teach your daughters to cower in height so that she does not overtake her brothers or show figure?
Is she to be sexualized in her kingdom and home?
Blood of mine, why do you teach your daughters submission to a harsh tone and cruel voice?
Are you threatened by her power already?
Blood of mine, why do you teach your daughters to feel fearful of the blood that visits every moon?
It is the only blood that isn't drawn by hatred or anger.

Blood of mine, did they teach you these things as well?
Did they make you hate your womanhood?
Did they taunt you for budding, sprouting and blossoming into one?
Do you see a reflection of yourself when you look at your daughter?
Is this why you hate her too?

—

The bitter seeds of Mother Pomegranate are not more bitter than I am.

—

Do you know why the woman wears black
to the graves of those that
were once men dressed in flesh?
Or why the unborn at her womb
no longer feeds off her body from inside
and returns to dead matter once more?
There is some trauma holding itself
underneath those obsidian eyes
in the shape of crescent moons upon her face;
She does not sleep nor rest.
She does not turn to face you in your words.
Do you know where the bodies go
after a holy man claims there is no longer life
between the lungs?
The woman sends it to the grounds below
for it to be forgotten along with the legend
of a devil hungry for more souls
For his dead kingdom within the trenches.
She lies here in the sands of her time,
both literally and metaphorically,
stargazing in the light of the sun,
unhappy because she does not see any stars.
It will take a woman eons to learn that the stars and the strongest
tide come out only when the world falls pitch black before her eyes,
and that only the purest of art and understanding comes from seeking a light
within that specific darkness.
Until then, she sits on the shores of Asahi bay wondering why death
had followed her everywhere and taken things that mattered most
even though it shouldn't have.

—

I imagine there was another me somewhere before I came to be in this world,

I imagine she would have many words for me

On how to make it around and alive on this Earth

I imagine she would tell me that if I was able to do so,

To try to rage and storm the Earth

And then to swaddle every baby and make them laugh at least once before I depart

I imagine there was another me somewhere before I came to be in this world,

I imagine she would have many warnings for me

On how love was written only to give women hope

Past the confinement of their homes

And that if I really wanted to be cared for,

No amount of children or lovers would be able to grant me that luxury

Because a woman only has the love she puts forth at the end of the day to tend to her.

But she is strong.

She *is*.

I imagine there was another me somewhere before I came to be in this world,

I imagine she would look at me and smile

because I did not have to suffer and crawl on hot coal like she did

Or like her mother did

Or her mother before that

And their hearts would feel free as doves seeing that I get to choose who I want to be

And that I'm the closest womankind or my bloodline has ever been to *freedom*.

—

Dear Troubled Woman,
There is no "one size fits all" in life.
Joy, Love, and Power take many forms—
(You are one of them)
Run with your palms open to the Earth.

—

Little girl–
how does it feel to never have enough space to
stretch your arms,
To run wildly,
To jump from the ocean rocks,
To climb the trees,
To swim with the waves,
To fly with the hawks,
To watch the sun *set*,
To watch the sun *rise*,
even though they told you that the stars,
mountains, oceans and Earth
were all *yours* to roam and dance with.
How does it feel to have been offered everything
from the birth of your being,
To have been told fairytales and myths
Of a woman's freedom
But to then have your wings clipped
To have your soul caged
And to be called names and things created to *only*
defile a woman.

They used to only tell us lies.

—

The most beautiful women in the moment are always the ones that remind us of the softest parts of ourselves with their art.
So when the chorus belts sounds that are deep enough to move mountains,
May the world know it is my voice carrying the power to do so.
May the world know that not only do I sing for the Earth, to mend its pieces,
but also give from my flesh as well when it is missing something.
All artists make sacrifices.
And for great women, they do not know their limits.
May the world one day look at at each of us with wonder and beguilement in their eyes
the same way our loved ones do.
The same way the mountains do when you mend their rocks.
The same way the ocean abyss does when you fill the trenches with light.
The same way the clouds gleam down on you when you relieve them of the burden of their sorrows.
Continue to be great.
The Earth is waiting for more of your harmonies and melodies that have yet to come.

—

You will have to ask Calypso about the years she spent alone
And how they made her a deity because of it.
Glamorizing a woman in her sadness and heartbreak
after being abandoned by many that stopped by her home.
Then made her into the image of a damsel in distress
which undermined the efforts of both Calypso
and the great women
that carried on after her.
You will have to ask Calypso of the water that holds her home–
And how man tried to breech her shores
And how she captured each one underneath her waves
And took them as her own.
Stuck in the glass of her blue waters,
On display for the world to see what happens,
When you mockingly place too much honor in a woman that craved love
And then depriving her of it
For the sake of your stories and tales.

—

The woman who blossoms into her Light Feminine Energy
does so after discovering her footsteps again,
You will see her take notice of how her weight presses into the ground
and leaves a print behind,
yet her feet still go with her.
She now understands that she is a traveler passing through.
Her mission becomes leaving a story,
a lesson or some form of goodness anywhere she goes,
to show the Earth
that the weight of her existence means something.
She laughs loud enough so the old folk can remember what youth feels like in the echoes.
She dances on soft floors,
Tripping over her shoes so the ground feels more pressure from her joy above.
Joy, by the way, is now hers.
Grace is hers.
Humility is also hers.
All women shall reach their time.
Even if their time now is dull,
We never remain dull.

—

You're an old shell I'd like to keep.
The cracks at the edges
remind me of your broken surface
and how strong you have been for so long to remain a whole.
You once held a pearl,
I'm just curious to know who stole it.
Did they have to lie to you for it?
You're still a pretty shell and you'll always have a home here by my shore.

—

A desert rose knows where to grow because she only blooms where rain is sure to come.
Flowers know where they will be appreciated the most.
Just like the dirt knows when to turn to mud when the monsoon hits–
soil and water have always danced well together.
And she will know which soil will kiss her roots the sweetest.
A desert rose knows where to grow her thorns so that no snake coils around her
and defames her name in the desert by calling her *his flower.*
Just like the hawk soars against the direction of the wind to show the power of its wings,
she grew from rebellion and learned to blossom in it.
Oh Desert rose, you grow in a no man's land
Yet you cannot hide from a travelers' taste for livelihood and danger.
One day, you will be plucked from the dry grounds you grew to love.
The stories of your rebellion, beauty and strong roots
will then just become stories for the desert
to blow away in the wind.
And the rain will come looking for you,
"Where is my Desert Rose?
I have come to water her in these hard times."
And the soil will call for your roots,
"Where is my Desert Rose?
I have come to hold her in these hard times."
And the wind will say,
"Leave her be, she has gone where flowers do not come back from,
But recite her name and tell the stories of her to celebrate the space she once took–
She was our Desert Rose."
The rain bellows, "She was our Desert Rose."
The soil cries, "She was our Desert Rose."

—

Woman in the tree,
whose trunk has swallowed your figure,
whose roots have grown deep into the ground with your soul in mind,
They told me you have been around here for over a century
Guarded,
and guarding the women who wander these forests.
They told me you gave up the life which would have made you a wife of a desirable man
and the mother of righteous children
Just so you may guard the women who travel these roads,
So they do not learn of danger the way you have.
They told me you watch the evil that linger in these forests,
And make holes in the Earth so that they fall through
Stuck in the trenches of their own wickedness,
So that another woman may never know of danger the way you did.
Woman in the tree,
whose leaves decorate your raven hair
whose branches stretch to touch the rays of the sun that wake you every morning,
They told me the danger you encountered in these roads,
How the devils took apart your heart and wore it around their necks,

How the gargoyles took apart your mind and flew great heights to watch it fall and laugh,
How the trolls took apart your body, leaving you to question your worth.
And how your remains sat beneath the shade of a tree
And as it rained the days after that, you became the water the roots took in
And your figure filled the trunk of the tree
Growing into Mother Maple,
To protect and watch over these women,
So that they may never feel heartbreak, insanity, and insecurity the way you did.
In the Forest of Madness.

You are of high value without the grand display,
    But a display we will give them anyway.

Oh love,
The moon holds her breath waiting for you to realize
She is the home that us women have forgotten about
The woman does not know her own glory yet
Till she knows the nature of the moon,
The tides she pulls to shore closer and closer
are only there to reach for you my love,
And to bring you back to her.
You have forgotten the power you both carry.
The women before you knew of it,
They owned it, carried it, and made themselves more beautiful with it.
They stood in council amongst each other,
Became leaders because of it,
Fought wars with it,
Became disciples in places of worship with their power–
The moon holds her breath waiting for you to realize oh love,
She is the home that you have forgotten about.

—

Dear Strange Man–
[There is a special kind of love with you in this home by the shore.]

هناك نوع خاص من الحب معك في بيت الشا هذا

ساحل کے اس گھر میں آپ کے ساتھ ایک خاص قسم کی محبت ہے۔

He has often said that even in my silence,
He feels me calling to him as a siren would.
Except, there is no danger that follows pursuit—
just home.
I am no siren of the sea
But I am the force that brings the tides close to shore
Reaching out again and again
To remind him my love is always pouring.
I am the caretaker of the sea as well,
It is my womb that calls out to him.
Man is surely made of water and clay
And while their mothers carry them in the womb,
They too suspend in her belly in fluid made from her.
So yes,
It is my womb that calls to him
and he feels greatly for it.
And his feet shake the ground
running towards it,
To hold me again.

—

How rich is it Strange Man,
That you've shown up at the times I needed you the most
And disappeared the times I needed myself the most.
Strange Man,
There is no face of yours recorded.
For every woman has experienced the mystery of our own
Father Wound
a hundred times in you.
You are no man solid,
But still somehow– you show up as every man we come
across.
Our hands are empty, Strange Man
But I assure you my heart is now brimming with joy
in its fullest capacity
with herself.
Leaving the Father Wound six feet under the ground,
where the rest of *him* is.
Who knew I would grow up in a world
that made livelihood so revolved around the idea of you,
Strange Man
and that there would be so many women who still cannot put
a face to your name,
But we flourish in our own
And on our own.

Without you.

—

Dear Strange Man,
In all the homes I've been in, slept in, laughed in and cried in
The fear of a man's anger has always hung over our heads.
Which man, I do not know.
It is this familiar fear of a man's wrath that we are all wary of.
The one that causes our breath to fluctuate,
Our hearts to race from the feeling of instability,
The one that makes us cower from danger.
Dear Strange Man,
In all the homes I've run away from,
The fear of a man's failure has always followed me.
Why does the failure of a man weigh so heavily over his family's shoulders?
That they pick up the pieces and feed themselves the shards
Yet still carry his last name when they make it out of the ruins to become something for themselves.

—

To the bones that dwell in Limbo,
find haven in a hurricane or storm that has not yet crossed your seas.
This is my eulogy to you,
as I never had a chance to sing these words
when your life was true to the flourishing rains
of the sky above.
It is the sharp greens of the wild that tend to my livelihood
The heavy folds above your eyes that prevented you
From seeing the things that made me happy when you were around.
The fresh air of the jungle intertwine
with the raw aromas of Earth
and you lie wasting away in stagnation
as if the wonders of the Madre Terra would just find its way to you–
When you were supposed to run towards her with your arms wide open.

O Love,

There was a time when I looked forward to coming home to you.

But now this home only needs me.

—

Jaan,

Women who come from shattered homes do not know what it means to feel protected,

But under your arms do I learn that feeling and meaning so well.

There are thoughts I cannot bring myself to find the words for

in fear that I may be exiled for the errors I may make when speaking,

But in your presence do you translate and interpret the things that are hidden in me,

and an open book I become.

The tragedy of love is that

it brings out the terrors *the child* once had,

Growing up in a home that was binded by chaos, disorder and hatred.

Although most healing should be done outside the boundaries of a union,

some old wounds, *child-like wounds*

are meant to be cured with love at your side,

because although love provokes them,

it also softens and salves the wound once you learn of its origin,

and how to alleviate the burden it has placed on your back

when you were only *just a child*.

—

He told me my desert eyes had no end,
and it was only till today did I learn that it meant
that he did not know where Madre Terra stopped
or where paradise started
when our gazes met–
And when our hearts met.

—

If my father had his own book,
his own verses or scripts
Written by me–
What would be the names of the chapters in that book?
Fragility of Petals
Apprehension of Hell
Decay of the Apple
Succinctness of Love
Tiers of Fatherhood
Ignominy
Heartbreak
In Another Life

I did not know
that even in love could someone take me apart
And turn me into little pieces
And expect me to wait for them as *One* again.

Well, I am not *One* anymore.
I am a thousand hurting.
I am hundreds curled up in their many shells by the river.
I am tens and tens of thoughts of heartache racing through the woods.

And if I am to be One for anyone,
It would be for myself, Strange Man.

You, I and God know that I need myself again.

—

The same moon my love,
In which your grandmothers and grandfather loved under
will still be there for our children
for them to love under as well.
It is she, the moon
That stays the same to remind us
that love is the one thing
that ensues, eon after eon
expressing itself in multiple ways throughout the years.
We've loved so much–
That we are predisposed to it.

And so I know,
I will be with you in every life.

I do wonder what was the look
on Adam's face
When he first saw Hawa (Eve)
And the human phenomenon of that love-gaze becoming a
genetic print on all of us.

May I know the name of the person who took the rock from beneath
my body,
that caused me to lose the strength of my limbs below,
allowing my collapse?
May I know who took my bones
And left me spineless
Snatching the voice from my throat
Allowing for dismissal and oblivion of my existence?
When stars are born
They do not meet their doom till eons have passed
So why is it when I felt I had been rebirthed through meeting you,
I met my doom and collapsed shortly after?
Dear Strange Man,
Do you awaken a woman's love
With no intention of catching her?
So that she falls continuously
Just as a star would in the void of space?
A dying star does not go out without a Supernova event,
Demanding that all of space stops and admires the hope that once
bubbled in her,
So the hope that once bubbled in me,
And kept my livelihood going will not go out without a show
It will expand, bubble, erupt in the colors of black and red,
In the colors of love,
And because my love and hope was too large to contain,
The death of me will have left behind a blackhole–
Now, Strange Man
May I know the name of the person who took the light and gravity
from beneath me,
that caused me to lose the strength of my celestial being,
allowing my collapse through space?
I wish to return the favor through the new void I've become.

—

I once walked in on the Strange Man,
And for the first time
I saw him take his past and make art with it–
His paints each meant something before he drew his brush to the canvas.
The shades Trials and Tribulations were dark,
The prints they made were like graphite sketches on concrete walls.
Calamities and Misfortune were long streaks
of dull colors that corrupted the white wash tones.
Idleness and Paranoia were the worst shades to paint with but he used them anyway.
The Artist,
with all his experiences,
 knew they weren't going to outshine the beautiful hues of Joy and Grace.
The stunning tones of Desire and Commitment tied the mess together
and Passion topped it off and made His Work a masterpiece.
After careful thought, He decided to name it "Life".
Because in the end, The Strange Man decided that His Life is what He decided to make it
He was only a couple decades late in realizing that —
and I'm so happy I could see him be proud of himself for the first time.

—

I thought that my greatest love
will be the one in my head.
The person that almost could never come to life beyond
the borders of my mind.
Or perhaps I am confining myself to one image.

I will admit though,

I also do not know what is good for me.

Dear Strange Man,
You've saved me from myself time and time again.
In my deepest moments do you take me away from the burden
of being alive for so long
And the dread of not having no fruit to bear
Or no rewards to call my own.
Dear Strange Man,
You have made life a little less burdensome for me,
Laughing with you
takes the weight of so many years (that I haven't lived yet) off.
And you know what is the best part?
I believe myself to be in the year 2050 when I'm near you–
That you know every curve, thought and bone that aches me.
That you know what makes me smile, rejoice and will give me tears of joy.

May my Dunya and Akhira be with you.

—

Be greedy with love,
If he is the one for you,
He will meet your greed with a monsoon.

Dear Strange Man,
You have taught me that if I am to be loyal, loving and a mother to anyone
It should be myself first
Before it is anyone else.
I could never bring myself to speak these words because I know of the limitations present
since you are a man
And that you are are self serving–
So how could you understand?
You do not know how badly I wish I could have been my own mother,
Or a mother to my mother
You do not know how badly I wish to have been my own lover,
Because both I could not trust
What are the chances that I was put at the mercy of both?
And that I would spend a lifetime unraveling the hurt and wounds that each
have caused me.

—

Jaan,
When my soul had a place on this Earth a few centuries ago
Where the tales of Asahi and her love story spread far and wide,
The first signs that showed our people
that we were connected to our lovers
through a red invisible string
was first observed from us.
The village often looked longingly at us and wondered why our love had occurred
In the times of hardship and dismay,
And the truth was Jaan,
That in every life {if there were multiple},
That you would always find me even if we were two specks in an abyss.
That even if the trees and our homes were burned to the ground,
You would find me
Whether I was beneath the soil or curled on top of it.
Mama told me to not underestimate the myth that lovers by fate are bound by *the red string*.
And that the little boy you once were in your village,
Who must've crossed the same roads as I did
Would have no idea of the storm that would hit him
When he finally meets with her.

Jaan,
You follow me at the hip.
And I am attached to you at your rib.
Do not forget this.
Do not forget this.

My Love,
A million times over and over and over again for you.
If I could lift your heart up from the pain my mistakes have caused you,
If there was ever a way,
I'd run towards it with open arms
And as fast as my legs could take me,
Hoping that stepping on hot coal,
Running under bridges that aren't mine,
Through storms that I did not cause
Would make you feel a little better
Because my dedication to love is stronger
Than my need to be right.
So for you,
I may keep putting myself away
Just so you feel you have more room in this forest
And to hopefully forgive me for things that were beyond us.

{I hope we do not hurt forever over this}

—

Dear Man in the Tree,
How does it feel to hang so low
That your feet touch the Earth
Yet you still call and cry that Death is chasing you
When the Woman in the Ground
is Six feet below
Dirt in her mouth instead of words,
because Death has caught her
and embraced her instead.

You were not kind to her.

Godspeed, My Love–

[I have found you, O Faith, a hundred times and I will find you a thousand more.]

لقد وجدتك أيها الايمان مئة
مره وسوف أجدك الف مره

اے ایمان، میں نے تجھے سو بار پایا ہے اور میں تجھے ایک ہزار بار تلاش کروں گا۔

Dear Creator,
I have not seen the end of the world,
I have not been far or wide,
I have not reached for the clouds above me,
Even though they are within distance,
Even though the voices far and wide are asking my name,
Even though the end of the world is calling for me.
I dare not ignore the world you created for me any longer,
The world you created for the men and women before me.
For the children that are yet to grace this Earth.
I have pushed these blessings away too long,
And there is a part of me that will always have regret for that
Regret for not enjoying the world you've laid at my feet.
The end of the world is calling for me Oh Almighty,
In this world of yours that does not have any edges,
That is endless in structure,
Spinning with blessings.
Why have I confined myself to the walls of my little home?
When you have told us we are given all this room to pray,
Knees and head to your exaltation.
The desert, the roads, the forest grounds,
Has only given me more room praise you,
Yet I have not prayed as much as I could,
I have not ran far or wide enough to see what else awaits my little mind.
I am coming,
let it in be my Naseeb (Qadr, Fate) that I will no longer keep myself small,
And I will roam the Earth and make something beautiful of myself in your Name.
I am coming Ya Rabb (O Lord).

—

Faith,
I have served you for decades—
but it was only of recent did I wake up and see
how soft you really are.
O My Faith,
There is a time in every human's life do we wake up out of the habit of practice,
And see you as something that is synonymous with Joy and Peace.
The people who have taught me about you were not soft,
Nor did they give me the joy and peace that should've came with
The teachings of Deen
But I have found it myself—
And I am here now
in the protection that you offer,
In the discipline that I am learning everyday.
Faith,
I have served you for decades—
But it was only of recent did I wake up and see
How soft you really are.

Ya Rabb, let me leave something good here before I go.
I know I am capable of doing great things.

(why does)
The western reign
continue to
open fire
on the dunes of my people
when there's already enough
flood and drought
in their bellies and soul?
The hunters
in silk black ties
bend their arrows
towards the children of
broken Syria
when they had nothing
to hide behind
except ruins
 of old shattered history
and rotting hope.
"How come mama,
the whole world gets to play
with their toys
and fire their missiles
while we sit here
with decaying bones
 at our feet
and a baby at your womb
who will be declared dead

as soon as you are to deliver?"
A child had asked me this
with empty eyes.
Children shouldn't play
with dead things
but here they are,
behind the tombstones
in Palestine
playing with dead hopes and dreams,
pretending they have a match strong enough
to ignite a fire
in their bellies
that would light up their future.
Why was the west so threatened
by the mirage
(in the midst of their greed)
of a woman with a scarf
draped over her head
in accordance to her culture
and belief?
What was so horrifying
at the sight of her
overcoming the pressure
of a wild culture
where women were objectified
and sexualized
by the glamor

men paid for on screen?
Where did their black money go
after they left the hands
of the men who believed
everything they touched
turned to gold?
There were people on this side
of the world too,
where they sent their drones
and fighters to bleed out
the rest of the cattle.
there were hopes and dreams
on this side too,
where they sent their minimal aid
to compensate the damage
that broke into their very homes
and the hearth
of their soul.
There was love and light on this side too,
where they sent their hatred and destruction
to overturn whatever happiness
that was left dancing with their souls.

—

Dear God,

I run towards my Qadr (Fate)
That ammi said was written for me.
I run towards You,
With oysters and pearls in my hand
grateful for the waters that wet my feet,
which You turn into clouds over the oceans, seas and rivers
and shower our fields
feeding us our earnings
That we've waited all year for.
I do not know what my Qadr is
But I know that I must dance where my feet will get messy,
I know I must find praise for you and pray when times are hard,
I must walk where I know will be far beyond my own imagination,
To reach the Fate that was written for me
years before Creation was made,
I do not know what is in the Realm of the Unseen,
But I know You wrote my Fate there,
So I will walk,
I will soar,
I will dance,
With my feet in the waters,
Till I get there.

I never understood forgiveness
Till I stepped back and saw
The hands of my own
That were red and blue with guilt
Till I stepped back and thought
'What if My Lord does not pardon me
For this sin that weighs heavy on my hands
and is flowing through my blood?'
But how can any deed be bigger than Your Mercy?
If You forgive me,
I may be able to forgive myself,
If you forgive me,
I may be able to forgive him.
I may be able to forgive my mother
And my sweet father
I may be able to look over the hurt of many things.

But forgiveness does not mean excused–
Although My Lord may has forgiven me,
What am I doing to refrain from defiling myself again?

―

Life blossoms somewhere on Earth
Even if they are not here.
The dead cannot taste salt tears where they are from,
So I will not shed any–
But I will tell the life sprouting from beneath the Earth
That I know who they each really are
That they are our loved ones peaking through for another smile
That the clouds rain when our loved ones miss us
from the homes they have in the sky
that the Earth trembles and shakes
when a child misses their mother
who went to visit the clouds years ago,
and never came back.
Sweet Zehra,
I hope you show the world the love you carry in your heart
because it now has no place to go.
because grief left you with a funny little hole,
that you found is only filled
when you empty yourself again and again
to give life and love endlessly
to everyone but yourself.

—

There is so much ugly when going through a spiritual awakening,
I do not look in mirrors on those hard days.

—

I'm going to cure myself.
Fast for forty days,
wear solid colors,
step outside to meet the Sun and the Moon at their given time.
Make a better home inside me because the one I live in doesn't bring me much comfort or joy.
I'm going to leave a bucket on my balcony and pray...
Pray till the weather warms a bit and the rains flower the riverbanks of Asahi.
I will drink that bucket water;
Have a taste of whatever entity is above and thank God for the nourishment because my slim body needed it.
I will stretch the depression and tears away on these lazy mornings and not feel sorrow, shame or guilt for the feelings of freedom the night before that made my heart and body quiver with hope.
I'm going to pray and I was told prayer doesn't always require a God, I was told,
"You can be your own God if you want too but in the end, when your hands no longer can raise up to the clouds in supplication because you're coffin deep in dirt, you'll have to answer to the Only God."
I'm going to dip my body in the hot spring waters and walk out glowing, feeling alive and awake because I will have let my anger wash away then.
Cure yourself.
Take three hours in a day, each sometime in the morning, evening and night and take a mental break. A deep breath, Stay away from people in those hours, call them your wake hours.
Then at every other time of the day, smile more, reach out a helping hand, write a little poetry and in no time my love, you'll be a blossom.
It just takes time for the buds to open.
I'm going to cure myself, just you watch.

—

Ya Rabb,
I am just a collection of fleeting moments
and experiences.
I am every moment that did not happen yet,
So forgive me when I run with my arms open towards the
things that are not good for me.

I still fear missing out on moments that could have been.

—

The flowers over this grave,
the ones blooming in our favorite colors,
tell me that every little thing fights for life—
that with their little bodies, they fight to live.

And that life always finds a way.
The death of one is never the end of it all—
It is usually the beginning of much more, many more.
Not because I am better without them here on Earth with me
But because all the *love* I had for them
Now has more places to go.

But they will always be in my heart.

Just like flowers grow over the heart of the dead,
I too have learned to blossom after my period of grief and gray.

Death is never easy,
even though it's happened repeatedly for eons.

Still, a child cannot grasp what exactly is "gone"
when they first hear that one day their parents will grow old
and return to the ground where they cannot reach each other again.

But you can still laugh with their souls,
And smile at the flowers.
They are there to remind you to still fight,
And that they are here fighting by you for another day.

—

God comes in one form but goes by many names.
We appear in many forms, showing up as our parents, our
children, the people we admire and adore–
but were given only one name
– to recognize the chaos and mess that each of us are.

There are many books waiting in me,
To be brought forth on pen and paper
So that I may tell the world of my journey with God
And how I each time I have reached a hand out,
He has met me at an arm's length.
When I have reached an arm out,
He met me twice the length.
And every time I have fallen,
Prayer was still there–
And that I do not have to go through another human
To speak with Him, The Almighty
Because I am refined, pure and human enough to speak to Him
From the comfort of my home,
With the desires and wrath picking at my heart.

I'm sure He knew who we were when He created us.

—

To remain or become the person you are
Despite the doings of every evil that was made to tear you down,
It is Remarkable.

—

Dear God,

I know why one of your names is Self-Sufficient.
In the night when *sleep* crawls over to try to soothe me,
but my body cannot accept it
and my heart is aching from the many things I have
faced that day,
You are close, listening to the strings of my being strum
with *Sorrow*,
who is playing her hand.
You are not tired, You do not rest.
You do not beget nor were you begotten.
But You are what I may need.
Where I lack, where I am breaking, where I am hungry
or tired
You remind us that You are,
And that you have always been
And that You will always Be.

—

Surely there was some wisdom in saying that this life is an
illusion and a prison for the believer,
But while the good times are here,
I hope I am too,
Even if my time here is brief.

—

I know you take good people away,
I know we learn of death very early, Ya Rabb
I know that even though we experience death a hundred times,
We could never quite grasp how much of a hole it leaves every time we each think of a solid departure.
I am not questioning you–
I know mankind would hate to have to live for all of eternity surely
Because then where would the beauty of forever after lie when we speak of love and hope if it never ends?
But we know men and women far and wide would still seek legends of Eternal Life just to say they tried
To live up to this *forever after*
That deep down we will always dream of.

—

Do you believe that beauty in God's Realm remains constant like that of our world?
If you took a portion of the rocks and sand that fill the grounds,
You will see skin and blood in every color and taste.
There is compliance with the stones beneath our feet and the face and limbs we walk with.
How from one, comes many.
How from the golden dunes come the souls of the Amazigh tribe.
How from the black sands come kings and queens of Maasai.
From the burning brown soil, comes the light of the Gurang people.
The beauty from His realm does not come from the singularity of one people or the stagnancy of the sun hanging.
It does not remain constant like that of a picture but instead like a film.
Beauty is ongoing, everlasting, moving with the waves beneath napalm skies.
It is a perceived sense of differences even through familiarity
which is why love always exclaims that you're different–
Which is why he tells me I am different.
Which is why those who love us always looks at us with warmth and exclaim we are different from the rest,
That we are not constant and instead we are the erosion within a rock, turning and twisting and breaking again and again.
From the ties of beauty they laid upon us,
weighing us down when we live in God's Realm,
Where beauty is not constant but twirling and running
Swimming gracefully and still moving.
Till *she* is still.
There is beauty in you and everything around you.

Ya Rabb,

I know that all good things come to an end.
So I tried to tear the Earth apart.
I tried to wreak havoc.
I tried to spin the threads of my life with chaos.
So maybe then, I would have more time here.
Because good things leave us too soon.
More time to make mistakes, more time to cry, more time to love.
More time to believe, more time to repent, more time to *be*.

—

Dates, water, and faith.
A humble diet of a believer when he is in the state of worship.
But what about when he is in a state of despair?
What does he eat then to curb his sorrows, Ya Rabb?

صلاح صلاح صلاح

Namaz. Namaz. Remember your Namaz.

More faith will give him freedom but like a wise man once said,
tie your camel first.

If the Pomegranate falls ripe from the tree,
Alas, it is yours to take.
Did you think she did not know
that you were waiting for her to blossom and fruit
In your favorite hues of scarlet?
Old Tree,
Thank you for the decades of roots and seeds,
Roots and seeds,
Roots and seeds,
Infinitely giving me more of her.

I cannot get enough.

End.

About the Author

I, Zehra {ZEH- RA Translated to 'Flower' in Arabic}, am a Muslim Indian-American who was born in California, USA but was raised in New Jersey for the majority of my life. It was always a dream to publish a work of my own hoping that when I do put something out, it will find the right people. I have always struggled with finding the peace to give my art the full attention it deserved but this was the year I knew I needed to do great things for myself to be the woman I have envisioned to be since I was a child. I wish that every person I have ever met also understands the same beautiful things about themselves as well.

I've grown up in Jersey City, Paterson, Morristwon to now the shores and beaches of Central Jersey and I can say I have *lived*. I've seen what struggle is and I've also seen the blessings that I've been granted with. I am forever grateful for the opportunity given to me that allowed me to snatch the reins of my life to create my own story.

How that will end– I do not know.

But I know what things make me happy and the things I'm good at and can share with the Earth.

So here's to the beginning of a new chapter of my life.

Best,

Zehra Adil

Contact Information:
Email: asizrn.zehra@gmail.com

Made in the USA
Middletown, DE
24 December 2024